Money & ME
In God We Trust

Creating Positive Change

Sign me up!

Train the Trainer

Sara Money

About the Author

Sara Money was born and raised in Albuquerque, New Mexico. In 1992, she graduated with a Bachelor's of Arts degree in Psychology and Communications from the University of New Mexico (UNM). In 1998, she graduated with a Master's of Arts degree in Counseling from Webster University in Albuquerque, NM. She has worked and volunteered in many places, including Albuquerque Job Corps, NM Human Services Department (Income Support Division), Albuquerque Public Schools (Substance Abuse Prevention Program), UNM Agora Crisis Center, Albuquerque Shelter for Domestic Violence, and Albuquerque Rape Crisis Center.

Sara worked as the Executive Director for a non-profit - Love INC (*In the Name of Christ*) of Albuquerque a from 2011-2016. She was also the Albuquerque City Coordinator for the DeVos Urban Leadership Initiative (DVULI) located in Grand Rapids, Michigan from 2015-2016. She is now the CEO of the Money & ME, LLC Company.

Published by CreateSpace

© 2017 Money & ME, LLC 996618902

ISBN-13: 978-009966189-0-8

ISBN-10: 996618902

Money & ME: Train the Trainer

A Message from Sara

Who can survive on $1,000 a month? The reality is many people throughout the United States who are living on disability or earning minimum wage live on this amount. It is a struggle for people to pay for housing, food, and clothing as the cost of living increases in America. This increase is dramatically affecting the lives of low-income individuals and families. In July 2011, I was challenged to teach classes to low-income people on how to better manage their money.

My first attempt was to use money management concepts from proven financial literacy programs for middle-income people. I quickly discovered that low-income people were not familiar with terms like "vacations," "dry cleaning," and "life insurance;" using those words was like speaking another language. People with low incomes were familiar with acronyms like "TANF," "SNAP," and "SSI," which may be foreign to middle-income people. In addition to finding a new language, I discovered a new culture. It was interesting and exciting to learn cultural differences and discover a different world within my own community.

The *Money & ME Program* is designed to be simple, easy to understand, and help people learn how to take control of their money. If low-income people can learn and apply one of these concepts, they can begin the process of gaining control of managing their money. We have seen people save $300 per month when they stop buying chips, soda, and renting movies daily from convenience stores. People who have implemented the concepts we teach have been able to pay off money owed and have learned to live within their income levels. I realized that many people, such as those living on Social Security or disability, may always be considered low-income; none the less, I have seen the excitement when they realize they can have financial freedom.

Money & ME began with a basic budget worksheet adjusted to the language that low-income people speak. Now it is a complete workbook with PowerPoint and training. Many people helped in the development, including conducting extensive research and participating in focus groups. All the concepts and ideas taught are meant to be simple but life changing.

Money & ME facilitators need to understand the language and culture of low-income people in order to effectively help them. Volunteers from various professions have attended "Train the Trainer Team" classes to learn how to teach and coach these participants.

I invite you to become part of the *Money & ME Program*. You may become a Trainer, a Coach, or a participant. The important thing to remember is for *Money & ME* to be successful people must be willing to change their own habits and ways of thinking. You were created by God and He has a special purpose for you. I hope that you will walk with Him through this process to start a journey of making better choices that will impact your life for years to come.

Sara Money, Creator and Owner of Money & ME

Acknowledgements

From day one, this program has been a collaboration of many people, which included extensive research and focus groups. Each time the *Money & ME Program* was taught, things were added and improvements were made. Each person regardless of his / her role gave insight into the development of *Money & ME*. This program would not have happened without God's inspiration and the amazing people He brought together.

It is a pleasure and honor to thank the following people:

My family:
- My daughter, Cassie, who helped with childcare, editing, development, and teaching.
- My daughter, Emily, who inspired me to keep the *Money & ME Program* simple.
- My mom, Charlene Greenwood, for proofing worksheets, PowerPoint presentations, and curriculum, often late at night to help meet program deadlines.
- My aunt, Connie Ballenger, final editor.

Editors:
- Lauren Leggee, Love INC's Administrative Assistant, sharing insight into the low-income world, helping develop focus groups, and sometimes being "the focus group."
- Tori Pilcher, Love INC's Donation Center Manager and *Money & ME* Coordinator / Trainer, "pulling together" the many components, advising on redesign of worksheets, and revising content.
- Matthew Valerio-Hirschfeld, Ph.D., professor and advisor at Trinity Southwest University, assisted with scripture references and development.
- Glenda Austin, Administrator, Registrar at Trinity Southwest University, for her insight and assistance with graphic design.
- Paula Avery, Mike Henderson, and Yvonne Lara, Love INC's Writing Club, for feedback.
- Jennifer Hutchins, final editor.

Others:
- Edith Carreon, Love INC's Clearinghouse / Helpline Manager, for translating everything into Spanish and sharing insight into the Hispanic culture.
- Love INC's 2014 Board of Directors: Robert Voss, Anthony Lovato, Kevin Johnson, Steve Denning, and Terry Dwyer for their prayers and support.
- Mickey Beisman, attorney, who gave legal advice and encouragement.
- Mike Cosgrove, Executive Director of True North Financial Ministries, for sharing his knowledge and expertise of money management principles.

Table of Contents

Agenda

8:30	**Registration: Pick up Training Material**

8:45	Welcome and Introductions
	(People briefly introduce themselves)
9:00	Section 1: Overview
9:15	Section 2: The Audience

10:30	**Break**

10:45	Section 3: *Workbook Content*
	Income & Spending Worksheet
	Discussion: How did your parents handle money?

12:00	**Lunch**

12:30	Section 3: *PowerPoint Guide Introduction*
	Workbook Content - Workshop
	Activity: Cash Envelope System
	How to Create a Payment Plan
	I Can Change!

2:15	**Break**

2:30	Section 4: Logistics
2:45	Section 5: Need to Know
3:15	Section 6: Equipping the Coach
3:30	Section 7: Forms and Q&A

1

Overview

- Program Design
- The Audience
- Program Content
- Coordinating a Program
- Need to Know
- Equipping the Coach

Program Design

- There are many great programs written for people "with money." *Money & ME* is written for people with little money.
- *Money & ME* is a money management program designed for low-income individuals and families.
- It is written with inspirational quotes called "Words of Wisdom."
- It consists of a six one hour sessions. It can be done in a one day workshop or six one hour workshops or a combination.
- It is designed for organizations to help low-income people in the community to be better stewards of the money they receive.
- Trainers and Coaches must complete a comprehensive training.
- A good class size for the orientation and workshop is 15-30 people.
- The program is an overview to teach people how to take control of their money. *It is NOT a time to address more complex and specific issues.*
- Follow-up is an opportunity to meet with the participants one-on-one to teach, encourage, and address certain topics.
- Follow-ups should be scheduled at the workshop and should be held within 2 weeks after the program.

The Audience

- *Money & ME* was written for people who may have an average income of $12,000 / year.
- These people typically do not have bank accounts.
- These may be people who have been homeless, living on disability / welfare, or earning close to minimum wage.

Program Content

- The *Money & ME Workbook* has utilized many focus groups to learn the low-income language.
- Activities are designed to help participants think and learn for themselves. *(Trainers are facilitators and should not give direct answers.)*
- A variety of learning styles are incorporated into the program.

  - ➤ PowerPoint slides use pictures and animations to reinforce visual learning.
  - ➤ Trainers talk through the slides for auditory learners.
  - ➤ Activities are designed throughout orientation and workshop to assist tactile / hands on learners.
  - ➤ ALL activities are designed for low-income adults!

Coordinating a Program

- Coordinating a *Money & ME Program* is not magic.
- It takes money and people to make this work.
- This training will teach you how YOU can have a successful *Money & ME Program*.

Need to Know

- How to engage your audience.
- How to be professional.
- How to deal with different personalities.
- How to speak in front of a group: public speaking tips.
- How to deal with difficult situations.

Equipping the Coach / Mentor

- What is a Coach's role?
- Where should a Coach meet with participants?
- Who should a person coach?

2

Preparing for the Audience
- Low-income Culture
- Different Learning Styles
- Personal Reflection

Low-income Culture

It is important for people working with low-income individuals and families to be aware of language and cultural differences. There are activities throughout this section to help raise YOUR awareness of these differences. Without knowledge of the differences, a Trainer may inadvertently say and do things that may cause more harm than good. To help you learn more about the low-income culture, here are some suggested readings:

A Framework for Understanding Poverty: A Cognitive Approach
Ruby Payne, Ph.D

When Helping Hurts: How to Alleviate Poverty without Hurting the Poor...and Yourself
Steve Corbett and Brian Fikkert.

Entering a new culture

- How many of you have taken a trip to a different country?
- What steps did you take to learn about the culture?
- Think of a *Money & ME Program* as taking a trip to a foreign place.
- It's about relationships.

Activity: Low-Income Questionnaire

Work individually for a few minutes and then discuss in small groups (3 - 5 people).

How much does it cost to do one load of laundry at the Laundromat, including washing, drying, detergent, and dryer sheets?

_____

_____

_____

Where can people go to get quarters to do their laundry if their Laundromat doesn't have change machines?

_____

_____

_____

What are some of the reasons a low-income person will NOT have a checking account?

_____

_____

_____

What is the average monthly income for families attending the *Money & ME Program*?

_____

_____

Why do you think low-income people spend money on tattoos?

_____

_____

_____

Which utility would you pay if you can only pay one and why?

_____

_____

_____

Money & ME: Train the Trainer
2017© Money & ME, LLC All Rights Reserved

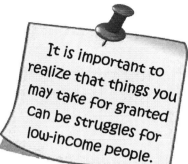

It is important to realize that things you may take for granted can be struggles for low-income people.

How often do low-income families take a vacation and where do they go?

_____

_____

What is a low-income family's source of entertainment?

_____

_____

Why do low-income people give money to a relative who doesn't work and neglect to pay their own bills?

_____

_____

What are payees? When are they used?

_____

_____

Where can you go to get food when you do not have money to buy food?

_____

_____

Where do you go to get clothes when you do not have money to buy clothing?

_____

_____

What are places low-income people might owe money?

_____

_____

Crossword Puzzle: Learning a New Language

Across

2. Supplemental Security Income
3. _____ Security Retirement, Disability or Survivor's Benefits
4. Temporary Assistance for Needy Families
5. Supplemental _____ Assistance Program
6. Acronym for federal program supplementing food for women, infants and children up to age 5

Down

1. Temporary _____ for Needy Families
3. Acronym for food stamp program
7. Electronic Benefits Transfer Card

Answers are found at the end of Section 2.

Keep it Simple

The Money & ME Program content teaches simple concepts to help people gain control not only of their finances but of other areas of their lives. For example, weekly meal planning, smart shopping tips, and ideas to stay in control of laundry are addressed. It is through these simple ideas with practical applications that make the *Money & ME Program* successful.

Help Participants Help Themselves

This program is designed for participants to learn for themselves. Through guided discussions and activities, participants recognize that they can make simple changes that become significant savings.

In the book, <u>A Framework for Understanding Poverty</u>, by Ruby Payne, Ph.D. she states:

> "One of the most valuable tools that educators can provide to students is positive affirmations. Completing tasks and learning something new is tied to your ability to self-talk your way through a task. If...then...statements are recommended. Find something the student can already do, and then say, 'If you can do this, then you can pass this test."

An example from Dr. Payne's book:

Three high schools boys failed a test four times. Dr. Payne knew the youth had the skills to pass the tests. She asked them if they had completed the tests, but they had quit in the middle, citing excuses such as being tired. Then Dr. Payne asked the boys if they had drivers' licenses. They did. Dr. Payne told each boy to tell himself if he could get a driver's license, he could pass this test. All the boys passed because they persisted.

The discussions and activities in the *Money & ME Program* help link new information to things participants already know how to do.

One young man put it this way, "Low-income people can look up and see middle class. But middle class do not look down and see how low-income people live."

Meal Planning

Imagine waking up hungry and not having any food in your home. You were at the grocery store last night, but you only bought what you needed for the day. Now, you need to go back to the store which takes more time and money. The *Money & ME Program* addresses creating a weekly menu to teach participants planning and organizational skills.

Smart Shopping Tips

The research with participants demonstrated that many participants did not understand price per ounce. They purchased the smaller quantity because it cost less. There are lots of shopping tips throughout the curriculum which include teaching price per ounce. It is important for Trainers and Coaches to understand that this is a new concept for participants that can save them money by looking at price per ounce or unit price.

Laundry Lessons

You wake up and have no clean socks, underwear, or clothes. Your children do not have clean clothes either. It is so difficult to carry everything to the Laundromat with your kids, and it costs a lot of money. Because no one has clean clothes, you decide to stay home and miss work and your children miss school.

Note: If people do not have control of their laundry it impacts EVERY area of their lives. It affects how they feel about themselves, what activities they do, and who they see.

Helping participants gain control over their laundry will have a positive effect over other areas of their lives. It will help their self-image, attendance at school and work, and their finances. This is especially true for women. When your laundry is out of control, your life is out of control. Through simple ideas, *Money & ME* helps participants gain control of their laundry.

Different Learning Styles

Low-income Learners

- Believe relationships are extremely important.
- Need an effective support group that incorporates authentic, caring relationships to deal with issues. *(This means leaders must be good listeners.)*
- Need to have belief, trust, and rapport to create the foundation required for long-term success.
- Use storytelling as their most common style of communication.
- Learn from stories and tell stories.
- Share stories that seem to go in circles and may not be chronological, but it makes sense to them.
- Appreciate the *Money & ME Program* because it is written in their language.

Patterns of Discourse

Discourse means how information is organized. In the formal use of English, the pattern of discourse is to get straight to the point. In casual speech, the pattern is to go around and around and finally get to the point.

Speaker or writer gets straight to the point.

Writer or speaker goes around the issue before finally getting to the point.

It is important for Trainers to realize that when they ask a question, it might take the participant a while to answer because of how his / her information is organized.

Visual Learners

- Think in pictures and learn best by visual images.
- Watch body language to help with understanding.
- Take notes.
- Appreciate the *Money & ME Program* because it is visually appealing through use of graphics throughout the PowerPoint presentation.

Auditory Learners

- Learn through listening and interpreting information by the means of pitch, emphasis, and speed.
- May not understand written language.
- Learn through repetition.
- May not be able to read or write.
- Appreciate the *Money & ME Program* because it is designed for the Trainer to verbally talk through each slide and important information is repeated.

Tactile Learners

- Learn best with an active "hands-on" approach.
- Favor interaction with the physical world.
- May have a difficult time staying on target and can become easily distracted.
- Appreciate the *Money & ME Program* because it has discussions and activities to engage these types of learners. DO NOT skip activities!

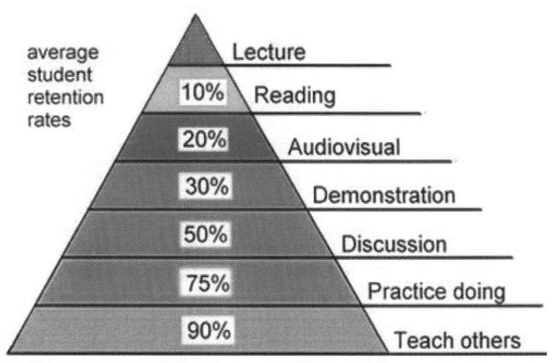

Learning Pyramid

average student retention rates

- Lecture
- 10% Reading
- 20% Audiovisual
- 30% Demonstration
- 50% Discussion
- 75% Practice doing
- 90% Teach others

Source: National Training Laboratories, Bethel, Maine

Money & ME is designed to maximize learning

- Fifteen to 20 minutes of lecture then activity.
- Discussions
- Games
- Practice doing.
- Teaching others!

Personal Reflection

Take a few minutes to write down your thoughts.

1. What surprised you about the low-income culture?

_____

_____

_____

_____

2. How will you use this information?

_____

_____

_____

_____

3. What else can you do to learn more about the low-income culture?

_____

_____

_____

Additional Thoughts

_____

_____

_____

_____

_____

Answers to crossword puzzle on page 14 :   Down 1. Assistance   3. SNAP   7. EBT

Across 2. SSI   3. Social   4. TANF   5. Nutrition   6. WIC

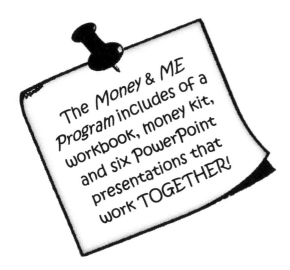

The *Money & ME Program* includes of a workbook, money kit, and six PowerPoint presentations that work TOGETHER!

3

Workbook Content

- Reality Check
- Responsibility
- Smart Shopping
- Build a Budget
- Plan for Money Owed
- Take Control
- Words of Wisdom or Scripture
- Information

Money & ME Workbook

The *Money & ME Workbook* is divided into eight sections. Sections one through six correspond with the PowerPoint presentations. Section seven includes scripture or "words of wisdom." Section 8 is resource information with a survey for participants to complete at the end of the program. The first activity participants perform is to put dividers in their own workbooks to familiarize themselves with the content.

Note: If you know you will have low-functioning or uneducated adults, it is recommended the workbooks be assembled ahead of time.

Money & ME PowerPoint Presentations

The *Money & ME Program* includes six one-hour PowerPoint presentations. Each slide has graphics and animations. Slides are designed for the presenter to use one click for each slide. Animations are timed for speaking and graphics come in at various times to help keep the audience engaged.

You design the program that works best for you:
- One day workshop – six hours
- Two sessions – three hours
- Three sessions – two hours
- Six sessions – one hour

Reality Check

GETTING STARTED

The first step is for participants to find their income and spending information. They will also need to find containers such as folders, boxes, or baskets to keep their information together. This worksheet guides them through the process of getting organized.

INCOME & SPENDING WORKSHEET

Participants need to record their monthly incomes and identify areas of spending. This worksheet has ten spending categories with graphics. This worksheet is the second step in creating a budget.

SAVINGS

This worksheets helps facilitate thinking about why it is important to save, different things to save for, and an amount that is good to have in savings.

NEEDS OR WANTS

Many times people think they NEED something when they actually WANT something. This activity helps participants identify what their needs are versus their wants. Participants enjoy the group discussions and learning from one another.

HOW MUCH DO YOU SPEND IN A YEAR?

Participants may not realize how much they are spending a year on something because they are buying it daily, weekly, or monthly. In this activity, they will write down every time they spend money to see how much it is costing them a year. There are 3 examples given, and then they do the activity. It is usually VERY surprising.

Responsibility

THINGS TO DO!

Everyone has things they need to do on a regular basis either daily, weekly, or monthly. Learning to take care of regular things will help prevent them from becoming a burden to themselves or someone else. In this activity they begin to identify and list their daily, weekly, or monthly responsibilities.

PLAN AHEAD

It is important for participants to see how stable their income is. Whether they work or receive disability or other monthly checks it is important for them to **PLAN AHEAD** for the unexpected. This will help them become more reliable employees.

SAVER OR SPENDER?

This worksheet and activity encourages participants to think about how they learned about money. What did their parents teach them about money? Were their parents spenders or savers? How are they similar or different? What are they teaching their own children? These questions help identify learned behaviors and how they can change.

HEALTHY OR UNHEALTHY HABITS

This worksheet AND discussion activity help participants identify healthy and unhealthy habits in a very general sense. Steps 2 and 3 engage them by asking why people have habits. Toward the end of the program there is a worksheet for them to identify a habit they would like to change.

Money & ME: Train the Trainer

Smart Shopping

HOUSEHOLD TIPS

Helping participants gain control over their laundry as well as utilize smart shopping tips will help them with their budgets.

HEALTH TIPS

Encouraging participants to eat healthy, take care of their teeth and get exercise will help them save money throughout their lives.

Keeping the instruction simple will help them be more successful.

CLEANING RECIPES

Many of the participants may receive food stamps or "Electronic Benefits Transfer-EBT." They may not be able to afford cleaning products, but they can buy lemon juice, baking soda, and vinegar with their benefits to make cleaning products. Here are recipes they can use to make cleaning products.

Also, this helps participants start to "think outside the box" and find other ways they can save money.

Make sure to tell them to label and date all cleaning products they make and store them out of the reach of children.

MEALS FOR THE WEEK

Helping participants plan their meals for the week will help them save money. Having a list of what they will need for the week will help them avoid trips to the grocery store. It will also encourage them to cook at home which is less expensive than eating fast food or buying food from a convenience store. One of the shopping tips is learning to look at the price per ounce. Many people buy the smaller item thinking it costs less. Once they realize buying smaller items is actually costing them more, they become smarter shoppers and get more for their money.

FEELINGS AFFECT SPENDING

Many times, people spend money because they are depressed, have addictions, low self-esteem, bad habits, when they are happy or bored. These feelings can put them into the "Money Owed Trap." The first step in changing is identifying a behavior. Talking about how feelings affect spending can help people change their behavior.

Money & ME: Train the Trainer
2017© Money & ME, LLC All Rights Reserved

Build a Budget

INCOME & BILLS CALENDAR

It is important for people to know when they get paid and when their bills are due. This is the second step in building a budget. Knowing when to pay bills will also help avoid late fees. This activity is done at home OR it can be done at a follow-up appointment. Remember, this is a workshop to give an overview of what they need to do. There is not enough time to actually do all the activities.

MONTHLY BUDGET

This worksheet is to be done AFTER the Income & Spending Worksheet and the Income & Bills Calendar are completed. Participants will decide how much from each paycheck they will put in each spending category. It is important for them to look at the monthly total AND the annual amount to see how much each category is costing them a year.

If they are spending more than their income, they will need to adjust the amount in their spending categories. If they are spending money in "wants" versus "needs" they can make changes. This can be addressed one-on-one with a Coach as well.

CASH ENVELOPE SYSTEM

This worksheet works with the money kit which includes an accordion file and ten envelopes. Participants will label their envelopes (inside and out) to correspond with the ten spending categories. These envelopes are where they will put their money when they get paid. They take the appropriate envelope with them when shopping. When they are out of money, they need to say NO!

SPENDING RECORD BY CATEGORY

This is a category ledger. It is very important for participants to use if they do use a bank account. It will help them to know how much they have in each category. If they use the cash envelope system, they can just look in the envelope. This ledger should match what is in their envelopes. They can use regular notebook paper as well. If a participant has a phone with internet, he / she could find an app to help him / her. Make sure the app doesn't cost them additional charges.

Money Owed Plan

MONEY OWED LIST

It is important for participants to list ALL money owed and the corresponding minimum monthly payments. This will be needed to complete the Income & Spending Worksheet and the Payment Plan. On the sample list, the participants will rank the amounts of money owed from least to greatest. This is how they will rank their money owed to create their Payment Plan.

People who owe friends or family may not be making regular monthly payments. Owing money could affect the relationship, and it is important that all money owed gets paid back to the lender.

PAYMENT PLAN

Have participants complete the Money Owed List and rank the amounts of money owed (excluding mortgage and car payments). They will re-write them on the Payment Plan starting with the smallest amount first. The participants will make the minimum payments to all the people and places they owe money. They will pay off the lowest total amount. Studies show that people need an "emotional win" to keep them motivated to continue paying off money owed. Once they have paid off one of the places or persons they owe money, they will use that amount toward the second smallest money owed. They will continue this process until all money owed is paid. The process is shown in the following pages.

The follow example show the concept of the Payment Plan, but does NOT include interest to keep it simple. The purpose of the example is to let participants know there is a light at the end of the tunnel (pay off Money Owed) if they complete this plan. When the last payment is made to a person or place, the allotted amount may be more than what is owed. The participant should add the full monthly payment to the next person or place owed the following month.

BOUNDARIES

It is important for participants to develop healthy boundaries in their personal life as well as how it relates to money. This worksheet helps facilitate the process.

EXTRA MONEY PLAN

When people receive extra money (gift, tax refund, inheritance, etc.), they usually spend the money without thinking about it. They forget to pay money owed and bills. This plan helps participants think about where they would spend their money if they got $1,000. This encourages them to think about percentages, but it is related more to "pieces of pie" – like a pie chart. Which piece of the pie should be bigger or smaller than others?

Money & ME: Train the Trainer
2017© Money & ME, LLC All Rights Reserved

Take Control

I CAN CHANGE

This worksheet helps a participant focus on one unhealthy habit he / she would like to change. Many low-income people are smokers. If they could stop smoking cigarettes, that would impact their health and finances for the rest of their lives. Each question will guide participants through a process of changing one habit so they will be able to have life-long change.

FUN ACTIVITIES

Participants are encouraged to think about activities they can do for free or that don't cost a lot of money. They write down their ideas, then cut out the activities into small pieces of paper. They can put these into a container and choose one when they are trying to think of something to do.

OTHER WAYS TO BE SUCCESSFUL

Most of the time when we think of wealth we usually think of money. However, there are other types of wealth.

- Relational Wealth: How are their relationships with friends, family and neighbors?
- Influential Wealth: Are they a positive or negative influence on others?
- Spiritual Wealth: You are not a human on a spiritual journey, you are a spirit on a human journey. What can they do to improve their spiritual self?

Words of Wisdom or Scripture and Information

WORDS OF WISDOM OR SCRIPTURE

Section seven is different depending on which version of the Money & ME you ordered. The Christian Edition has scripture and the Words of Wisdom has inspirational quotes.

Information

RESOURCES

Families who have a child on the free lunch program may be eligible for internet at $9.95 / month AND find other places to look on the internet for free activities.

FOLLOW-UP

Follow-up is a one-on-one meeting between the participant and a Coach / Mentor.

This worksheet will help guide Coaches when reviewing the material presented in the orientation and the workshop.

SURVEY

Each participant is to complete a survey at the end of the workshop and give it to the Assistant Trainer. This survey asks the participants how much money they owe (their debt), how they would evaluate the program, and what money management skills they learned.

These two forms will give you information on age, ethnicity, if they have a checking account or use a phone with internet, income level, amount of money owed, as well as what the participant learned. If you are applying for funding from other sources, this information is very valuable.

4

Logistics

- Best Practices!
- Protection of Participants
- Job Descriptions
- Resources Needed
- Scheduling
- Equipment
- Promotion

Best Practices!

The success of the *Money & ME Program* depends upon trained volunteers who understand their roles and how each job works together with other jobs. This program is simple but comprehensive. It requires a team of people to be successful!

- Trainer and Assistant Trainer understand their roles and work well together.
- Fifteen to thirty participants arrive on time ready to learn.
- Childcare workers who enjoy working with children, are familiar with the facility, and show up on time.
- Facility is clean and available one hour prior to start of the program.
- Host site staff is supportive of the *Money & ME Program*, leaders, and participants.
- Light snacks for orientation and a meal for workshop are to be provided by the host site.
- A volunteer clean-up crew is responsible for cleaning up, returning furniture and equipment as they were found OR making the facilities ready for the next function.
- Use technology that works (check before program)!

Protection of Participants

Lead Trainers, Assistant Trainers, and Coaches have influence over *Money & ME* participants. Some participants, because of their financial situation, may be vulnerable.

Therefore, as *Money & ME* leaders, it is important to protect the participants' interest. Trainers and / or Coaches must:

- Respect confidentiality. Do not share private information with others.
- Demonstrate ethical and professional behavior at all times.
- Fulfill the duties outlined in job descriptions.
- Complete Conflict of Interest statements (required).
- Disclose any potential financial benefit, such as investors or sales representatives, to the *Money & ME* Coordinator.
- Discuss how to avoid a potential conflict of interest.
- Do NOT use the *Money & ME Program* for personal gain.

Professionalism

- All information shared between participants and Trainer and / or Coach will be held confidential.
- Trainers and Coaches will demonstrate ethical and professional behavior at all times and fulfill the duties outlined in their job descriptions.

Background Checks

Each organization hosting the *Money & ME Program* will need to determine if background checks will be required for Trainers and / or Coaches. Check with your leadership and follow the appropriate guidelines.

Job Descriptions

It takes a team of people working together to have a successful *Money & ME Program*. The job descriptions help assist the organization with the various tasks and required skills to get each job done. The job descriptions are on the following pages.

Program Coordinator Job Description

Supervisor: Staff person in a leadership role at hosting organization.

Responsibilities:
- **Work** with appropriate staff to schedule dates, resources, people, supplies, facility.
- **Ensure** the facility has adequate classroom space for program, childcare space, equipment for children, and food preparation area.
- **Secure** Lead Trainer, Assistant Trainer and Childcare Workers for the program.
- **Ensure** training, background checks (if needed) and W-9's (if person will receive stipend) are completed for Trainers, Assistant Trainers, Coaches, and Childcare Workers.
- **Ensure** all necessary supplies are ready for each program including:
  - *Money & ME Workbooks and Money Kits*
  - Computer, clicker, batteries
  - Thumb drive with PowerPoint Orientation and Workshop Presentations
  - Projector and screen
  - Camera (for documentation of program and can be used for future promotion)
  - Administrative forms, paperwork and supplies

- **Confirm** with Childcare Workers, Lead Trainer, and Assistant Trainer one week prior to program to ensure they are still available.
- **Confirm** background checks have been completed if required.
- **Practice** with Lead Trainer.
- **Work** with hosting organization to help promote program.
- **Observe** Lead Trainer while presenting program.
- **Make** sure all paperwork is complete and submit to person responsible for stipend reimbursement.
- **Ensure** all participants are recorded in database (optional).
- **Record** program on the *Money & ME* website (*Program Support*).

Skills and Qualifications:
- Complete a volunteer application and background check (if required by host organization).
- Interview with staff leader of organization.
- Complete the *Money & ME* "Train the Trainer Team" training.
- Be able to coordinate people, facilities, and tasks in a timely manner.
- Be comfortable with public speaking.
- Communicate effectively on the telephone.
- Record client information accurately and legibly.
- Have basic knowledge of the internet and ability to perform basic search functions.
- Listen, empathize, and accept others while using discernment and a non-judgmental attitude.
- Establish and maintain personal and professional boundaries.
- Work independently and cooperatively - Teamwork.
- Commit to work when scheduled and be punctual.

Lead Trainer – Teacher Job Description

Supervisor: *Money & ME Program* Coordinator

Responsibilities:

Prior to program:
- **Complete** "Train the Trainer Team" training and necessary paperwork.
- **Work** with Program Coordinator to recruit help in promoting the *Money & ME Program.*
- **Test** all technology prior to program.
- **Write** your "Trainer Stories."
- **Practice** the PowerPoint presentation with equipment you will be using.
- **Help** with room set up.
- **Familiarize** yourself with building facility to know where restrooms, childcare, emergency exits, kitchen, etc. are located.

During program:
- **Arrive** an hour early to ensure room is set up, technology is working, and to welcome participants to the orientation or workshop.
- **Facilitate** the *Money & ME Program* (orientation and workshop).
- **Engage** participants to learn and interact with other participants.
- **Maintain** order and control during sessions.

After program:
- **Make sure** rooms used are clean.
- **Restore** tables and chairs as you found them OR set up for next function.
- **Collect** all supplies, kits, equipment, signs, etc.
- **Return** all technology after program ends.
- **Return** all paperwork, supplies, kits, etc. to *Money & ME* Coordinator after program ends.

Skills and Qualifications:

- Complete a volunteer application and background check (if required by host organization).
- Interview with *Money & ME* Coordinator.
- Demonstrate effective public speaking skills.
- Maintain order and control of participants during program.
- Practice using the Cash Envelope System in one area (usually extra stuff) for 90 days.
- Become comfortable using the PowerPoint presentation.
- Listen, empathize, and accept others while using discernment and a non-judgmental attitude.
- Establish and maintain personal and professional boundaries.
- Work independently and cooperatively – Teamwork.
- Commit to work when scheduled and be punctual.

Assistant Trainer – Administrative Job Description

Supervisor: *Money & ME* Coordinator

Responsibilities:

Prior to program:
- **Confirm** with the *Money & ME* Coordinator the number of participants expected.
- **Pick up** money kits, vouchers, coupons, paperwork, technology (if needed) and other supplies from Program Coordinator 1-2 days prior to the program.
- **Call** participants 1-2 days before program to confirm they know the program location and ask if they will be requiring childcare. Note: *Children will be in childcare except nursing babies. No exceptions. Those 16 and over who actively participate are eligible to receive participation gifts.*

During program:
- **Arrive** one hour early to set up registration and put up *Money & ME* signs.
- **Sign in** Childcare Workers. Give instructions on filling out childcare sign-in sheets.
- **Sign in** participants, give name tags at each session. (Have sharpie available.)
- **Hand out** registration forms – orientation.
- **Collect** and make sure registration forms are filled out completely at Orientation.
- **Distribute** *Money & ME Workbooks and Money Kits.*
- **Write** participants' names on *Money & ME* certificates.
- **Check** the times while the Lead Trainer is speaking to keep program on schedule.
- **Evaluate** Lead Trainer to give positive feedback and constructive criticism (see form).
- **Call participants individually by name** to the sign-in table and show them where they will turn in their surveys (end of workshop).
- **Hand out** participation gifts and have each person sign for his / her gift.
- **Ask** each person if he / she would like to sign up for follow-up. Schedule appropriately.
- **Make sure** rooms used are clean and as you found them OR ready for the next function.

After program:
- **Collect** all supplies, kits, equipment, signs, etc. and return to Program Coordinator.
- **E-mail** photos or put on thumb drive and give to Program Coordinator.

Skills and Qualifications
- Complete volunteer application and background check (if required by host organization).
- Interview with *Money & ME* Coordinator.
- Demonstrate administrative skills: ability to complete forms neatly and completely.
- Attend a *Money & ME* "Train the Trainer Team" workshop.
- Practice using the Cash Envelope System in one area (usually extra stuff) for 90 days.
- Listen, empathize, and accept others while using discernment and a non-judgmental attitude.
- Establish and maintain personal and professional boundaries.
- Work independently and cooperatively – Teamwork.
- Commit to work when scheduled and be punctual.

Promotion Person

Supervisor: *Money & ME* Coordinator

Responsibilities:

- **Coordinate** with the *Money & ME* Coordinator to set up the date for the orientation, workshop, and follow-up. Make sure to work around holidays and events already scheduled at the facility. Allow a minimum of four weeks to promote.
- **Complete** *Money & ME* promotion flyers with the dates, location, and telephone number to call for registration.
- **Map** distribution area. Decide who you are going to invite and your target area.
- **Coordinate** with other volunteers to help invite participants.
- **Complete** PowerPoint slide if it will help with promotion.
- **Look** for other ways to promote (i.e. Facebook, radio, signs, etc.).
- **Don't stop!** If you are reaching out to people you do not know, you need to over invite.
- **Take** photos of event. (Great for future funding and promotion.) Check registration forms to make sure participants have given their permission to use their photographs.

Skills and Qualifications:

- Complete a volunteer application and background check (if required by host organization).
- Interview with *Money & ME* Coordinator.
- Have knowledge of how to use computer to complete and print flyers.
- Enjoy interacting and engaging with people.
- Listen, empathize, and accept others while using discernment and a non-judgmental attitude.
- Establish and maintain personal and professional boundaries.
- Work independently and cooperatively - Teamwork.
- Commit to work when scheduled and be punctual.

Childcare Worker Job Description

Supervisor: *Money & ME* Coordinator

Responsibilities:

- **Arrive** 30 minutes early for *Money & ME* orientation and workshop to ensure room is set up.
- **Familiarize** yourself with building facility to know where restrooms, childcare, emergency exits, kitchen, etc. are located.
- **Welcome** participants with their children.
- **Make sure** parent(s) sign in / out their children.
  - ➢ give name tags to children
  - ➢ be sure allergies are listed on sign-in sheet
- **Supervise** children during the *Money & ME Program* (orientation and workshop).
- **Engage** with children in appropriate activities.
- **Maintain** control and order with children during session.
- **Make** sure the room used is clean and as you found it OR ready for the next function.

Skills and Qualifications:

- Complete a volunteer application and background check (if required by the host organization).
- Interview with *Money & ME* Coordinator.
- Enjoy working with children.
- Engage and supervise children in appropriate activities.
- Listen, empathize, and accept others while using discernment and a non-judgmental attitude.
- Establish and maintain personal and professional boundaries.
- Work independently and cooperatively - Teamwork.
- Commit to work when scheduled and be punctual.

Coach Job Description

Supervisor: *Money & ME* Coordinator

Responsibilities:

- **Meet** with participants during scheduled times.
- **Call** to confirm appointments.
- **Be** an encourager.
- **Keep** contact log of phone calls, appointments and progress.
- **Complete** follow-up sheets and give to *Money & ME* Coordinator.

Skills and Qualifications:

- Complete a volunteer application and background check (if required by hosting organization).
- Interview with *Money & ME* Coordinator.
- Complete the *Money & ME* "Train the Trainer Team."
- Have administrative skills: ability to complete forms neatly and completely.
- Practice using the Cash Envelope System in one area (usually Extra Stuff) for 90 days.
- Able to listen, empathize, and accept others while using discernment and a non-judgmental attitude.
- Establish and maintain personal and professional boundaries.
- Work independently and cooperatively - Teamwork.
- Commit to meet one-on-one with participants when scheduled and be punctual.

Cost of Program:

The cost of the program varies according to the number of participants. The following is a sample budget. It does not include shipping or cost of space, clean-up fees, etc.

	Cost	10 Participants	20 Participants	30 Participants
Workbooks & Kits	Regular $50.00 Non-profit $35.00	$350.00	$700.00	$1050.00
Incentives – Participation Gifts	$20	$200	$400	$600
Childcare 2 workers @ $10/hour	$120	$120	$120	$120
Snacks (varies) and meal	$70 - $100	$70	$80	$100
TOTAL Without Other Expenses		$740.00	$1300.00	$1870.00

Grants

There are grants available in every community. Look online and see what is available in your community. Most grants are like extensive job applications. You need to make sure you answer the questions correctly. Here are a few ideas of other places to look for grants:

- United Way
- Walmart
- Online (there are lots of grant opportunities – check the internet)

Sponsors

Talk to businesses that might be interested in sponsoring a *Money & ME Program*. Let them know it is helping members of their community. Show them the *Money & ME* workbook, kit, and curriculum to let them know this is a comprehensive program. You may also show them the cost of the program based on how many participants you would like to have attend.

Incentives – Participation Gifts

- It is EXTREMLY important to have incentives to get participants to the program.
- Through trial and error we discovered a good incentive is a $20 voucher / gift card for food or gas. The higher the amount of the incentive, the more participants will attend.
- Call them a "Participation Gift."
- It is recommended to NOT give cash.
- Develop relationships with businesses to see if they are able to donate to your program. Love INC of Albuquerque developed relationships with local thrift stores to offer a one-time coupon for 50% off clothing.
- Think of other incentives that may be available in your community.
- Volunteers helping to promote the *Money & ME Program* should have a *Money & ME Workbook* and K*it* to show potential participants.

Distribution of Workbooks & Kits

Before orientation: Take a few calculators and pencils out of the kits for participants to share for activities during orientation. **DO NOT GIVE** the kits at orientation.

Give each person a workbook during orientation sign-in. The workbooks have tab dividers toward the back of the 3 ring binder.

At the beginning of orientation have participants put the tab dividers between the appropriate sections. Once this is complete, the participants can begin the activity of getting to know a new person if there is time.

Give each person a workbook during session one sign-in. At the end participants will:

1. Put their name tags on the front of their workbooks.
2. Return calculators and pencils. (*Trainers need to put back into kits.*)
3. Return workbooks to sign-in table.

DO NOT send workbooks or kits home with participants at the end of each class. Participants will need these materials for other sessions. If you give the participants workbooks and kits at the orientation they may leave them at home when they return for the workshop. The workbook and kit are also an incentive to complete the program.

At the end of the program, you can give the participants their *Money & ME Workbook and Kit*. These are now theirs to keep.

Snacks

- Eating snacks and a meal together is a great way to help build relationships.
- Participants may be hungry when they arrive. Meeting this need will help with learning.
- Healthy food is encouraged for snacks and the meal.

Childcare

- It is STRONGLY ENCOURAGED that hosting organizations provide FREE childcare so participants are able to come.
- Paying childcare workers a stipend will help to get good workers who enjoy working with children.

Not all childcare workers choose to take a stipend. Talk with your childcare providers prior to the program to make sure there is clarity regarding payment.

Scheduling

- Programs scheduled toward the end of the month are typically more successful. Low-income people usually have money at the beginning of the month so they do not feel they have a money problem.
- Avoid weekends that have holidays.
- Coordinate with the hosting organization to see how to best promote and implement the program.
- Allow at least four weeks for promotion.
- Think of how many people you are trying to have attend and remember you need to OVER INVITE!

Follow-up

If the hosting organization offers follow up:

- Decide ahead of time if your hosting organization will offer follow-up.
- Participants will schedule follow-up appointments at the end of the workshop.
- Follow-up days and times should be listed on the information flyer.
- Follow-up should be held at the same facility as the program.
- Schedule additional follow-up sessions.

Equipment

- Laptop computer and power cord
- Clicker
- Batteries for clicker
- Screen
- Projector
- Extension cord
- Thumb drive with PowerPoint presentation
- Camera (optional)

Practice

- Schedule time for the Lead Trainer to work with the technology person.
- Have the Lead Trainer practice with the technology and the PowerPoint prior to the program.

Promotion

Advertise at hosting organization

- Announcements / bulletins
- E-mail newsletter
- Video or PowerPoint slide
- Post on website
- Facebook

Encourage others to promote

- Invite others to help with childcare, food, flyer distribution, set-up / clean up.
- Conduct a flyer distribution in the immediate neighborhood.
- Post information at libraries, community centers, Laundromats (taping flyers on washing machines or dryers), schools (backpack mail), businesses, community associations, neighborhoods, etc. Use discretion when distributing flyers.
- Use flyers with tear-off tabs when posting on bulletin boards.
- Distribute flyers 10 days to two weeks before event.

Sample flyer one per page with tear-offs at bottom

FREE Program
Location

Address

Orientation
Monday
Date
Time

Workshop
Saturday
Date
Time

Everyone MUST
Register
Phone #

Notes, childcare
options, etc.

Participants learn how to:

- Become smart shoppers.
- Identify needs & wants.
- Use Money Kits.

Workbook

This *Money & ME* is
for low-income
adults who would
like to learn how
to take control of
their money.

Money Kit

Every participant will receive for free:

Workbook and kit valued at $24.95
Click here to enter text.
Click here to enter text.

| *Money & ME* Click here to enter text. Call to register. | *Money & ME* Click here to enter text. Call to register. | *Money & ME* Click here to enter text. Call to register. | *Money & ME* Click here to enter text. Call to register. | *Money & ME* Click here to enter text. Call to register. | *Money & ME* Click here to enter text. Call to register. | *Money & ME* Click here to enter text. Call to register. | *Money & ME* Click here to enter text. Call to register. |

Sample flyer of two per page

Free Program Location

Address

Orientation
Choose an item.
Date
Time

Workshop
Choose an item.
Date
Time

Everyone MUST Register Phone Number

Notes, childcare options, directions, etc.

Learn how to:

- Become smart shoppers.
- Identify needs & wants.
- Use money kits.

Money Kit

This *Money & ME* is for low-income adults who would like to learn how to take control of their money.

Participants will receive for free:

Workbook and kit valued at $24.95
Click here to enter text.
Click here to enter text.

We look forward to seeing you!

Free Program Location

Address

Orientation
Choose an item.
Date
Time

Workshop
Choose an item.
Date
Time

Everyone MUST Register Phone Number

Notes, childcare options, directions, etc.

Learn how to:

- Become smart shoppers.
- Identify needs & wants.
- Use money kits.

Money Kit

This *Money & ME* is for low-income adults who would like to learn how to take control of their money.

Participants will receive for free:

Workbook and kit valued at $24.95
Click here to enter text.
Click here to enter text.

We look forward to seeing you!

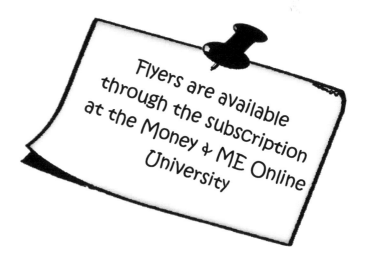

Flyers are available through the subscription at the Money & ME Online University

The flyers are created as a "fillable" word document. You can customize your own by putting in the location, date, time, address, notes, and incentives.

Program Review

It is important to schedule a debriefing time for the Trainers and Coordinator. Feedback from everyone is a critical part of this process. Make sure everyone has a copy of this program evaluation and completes it prior to the debriefing. Note: Not everyone needs to attend the debriefing, but everyone needs to complete this evaluation.

This time is to objectively evaluate how everything went with the goal for improvement for future programs. The evaluation covers the following:

- Facility
- Promotion / Attendance / Response
- Food
- Childcare
- Trainer
- Assistant Trainer
- Program Dates & Times

After the debriefing the *Money & ME* Coordinator can give positive feedback to the people who did a great job in their volunteer roles. For those who need constructive feedback, it is important to plan a time to speak privately with them. The *Money & ME* Coordinator should get help in this area if needed.

42

5

Need to Know

- Professionalism
- Dealing with Difficulties
- Dealing with Different Personalities

The *Money & ME Program* is simple, but it does require effort.

Section One encouraged Trainers to "Help Participants Help Themselves." Refer to page 16. This is also true for Trainers. Think of experiences you have had throughout your life. If you were able to handle (think of a situation), then you could handle something else that is similar. This section will help you prepare for situations that could happen.

Preparing for the unusual or difficult situations will help you have a SUCCESSFUL *Money & ME Program.*

It is hard to plan for every possible situation. However, there are things that happened while *Money & ME* was in development that we would like to share with you. This section will help you prepare for situations that could happen. Plan ahead of time!

Excerpted from A Framework for Understanding Poverty, by Ruby K. Payne. Copyright 2013 aha! Process, Inc. All rights reserved.www.ahaprocess.com

Professionalism

Arrive early:

- Visit the building ahead of time. Be familiar with the area where you will be conducting the program.
- Find locations of restrooms, childcare and emergency exits.

Dress modestly:

- You are a role model to participants.
- You are representing the hosting organization.
- You are to dress "one up" from participants. Business casual is OK.

Understand how to use equipment:

- Setting up the projector
- Setting up the laptop and PowerPoint
- Connecting the laptop and the projector
- Connecting the clicker to the laptop
- <u>Practice setting up ahead of time so Trainer is familiar with equipment</u>.

PRACTICE!

- Take the time to learn the material.
- Practice in front of a mirror.
- Practice using the equipment before the orientation / workshop.
- Use the program yourself.
- Write down your own expenses, use the Cash Envelope System for at least one category. The category "Extra Stuff" is a good category to record expenses.

Dealing with Different Personalities

The Lead Trainer may deal with difficult people in the audience. Listed below are possible personalities that you may encounter and tips on how to handle them.

Eager Beaver - Always the first person to participate and eager to help. He or she may make it difficult for others to respond.

- ➤ Do not dampen this individual's enthusiasm.
- ➤ Acknowledge his / her contributions and suggest that others participate.
- ➤ Have people raise their hands to answer questions.

Expert - Challenges your authority and argues with others.

- ➤ Get them on your side, use their expertise.
- ➤ Acknowledge his / her contributions and suggest that others participate.

Rambler - Can be a storyteller.

- ➤ Interrupt and summarize their comments and regain control.
- ➤ Ask for another person's opinion.
- ➤ DO NOT let this individual drone on.
- ➤ Agree to disagree so the rambler can save face.

Dominator - Wants to control and may intimidate the group by monopolizing the conversation or activity.

- ➤ Do NOT let dominators take over.
- ➤ Use humor to bring order back to the discussion.
- ➤ Call a break and speak to that person privately.

Money & ME: Train the Trainer
2017© Money & ME, LLC All Rights Reserved

Negative - Can be very resistant and create a negative environment. Speaks negatively about you or the subject. Does not want to be there.

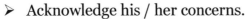

➢ Acknowledge his / her concerns.
➢ Let them know their feelings are important.
➢ Let them know they can come to a follow-up if there is something they would like to talk about.

Side Conversations - Happens when two or more people talk while you are presenting.

➢ Make eye contact with the talkers.
➢ Stop speaking until they look up.
➢ Walk toward them, stand in front of them.
➢ Ask them to stop speaking.

Complainers - Finds fault with everything, likes to whine but has no solutions. He / she is not necessarily negative about the subject matter, but likes to complain. This is the "Yes, but. . ." person.

➢ Do not get caught in their game.
➢ Instead, ask the audience for alternatives.
➢ Stay focused and move on.

Hecklers - Harass, challenge, or interrupt.

➢ Try to ignore them. If the person gets no response from you, he / she may give up.
➢ Walk over to this person.
➢ Do not show any hostility or use any put-downs.
➢ Ask them to step out of the room for a while.

Encourage Questions
➢ Make sure the question relates to what we are talking about.
➢ If the participant has a question or a big issue in his / her life or at work, ask participant to come talk after the class or schedule a follow-up.

REMEMBER: When dealing with difficult audiences your best strategy is a sense of humor. Disruptive behaviors are usually a symptom of an unmet need. Privately encourage people who demonstrate difficult behaviors to do follow-ups so they can have an understanding of what's driving this behavior. Get help from others as needed. Keep in mind we are not professional counselors – unless you are!

Money & ME: Train the Trainer
2017© Money & ME, LLC All Rights Reserved

Public Speaking Tips

OUR Advice: DON'T BE BORING

- Don't just read through the slides.
- Use different tones of voice, walk around a little, and interact with participants.
- Share personal stories where appropriate. CAUTION! Keep your stories short and on topic. Remember, there is a lot of curriculum to get through.

Additional Resources - Toastmasters.org

Feeling some nervousness before giving a speech is natural and even beneficial, but too much nervousness can be detrimental. Here are some proven tips on how to control your butterflies and give better presentations:

1. **Know your material.** Pick a topic you are interested in. Know more about it than you include in your speech. Use humor, personal stories and conversational language – that way you will not easily forget what to say.

2. **Practice. Practice. Practice**! Rehearse out loud with all equipment you plan on using. Work to control filler words like "ah," "umm," etc. Practice, pause, and breathe. Practice with a timer and allow time for the unexpected. Practice in front of a mirror.

3. **Know the audience**. Greet some of the audience members as they arrive. It's easier to speak to a group of friends than to strangers.

4. **Know the room**. Arrive early, walk around the speaking area, and practice using the microphone and any visual aids.

5. **Relax**. Begin by addressing the audience. It buys you time and calms your nerves. Pause, smile and count to three before saying anything. ("One one-thousand, two one-thousand, three one-thousand. Pause. Begin.) Transform nervous energy into enthusiasm.

6. **Visualize yourself giving your speech**. Imagine yourself speaking, your voice loud, clear and confident. Visualize the audience clapping – it will boost your confidence.

7. **Realize that people want you to succeed.** Audiences want you to be interesting, stimulating, informative, and entertaining. They're rooting for you.

8. **Do not apologize for any nervousness or problem.** The audience probably never noticed it.

9. **Concentrate on the message - not the medium.** Focus your attention away from your own anxieties and concentrate on your message and your audience.

10. **Gain experience**. Mainly, your speech should represent *you*— as an authority and as a person. Experience builds confidence, which is the key to effective speaking. A Toastmasters Club can provide the experience you need in a safe and friendly environment.

Engaging the Audience

It is EXTREMELY important for the Trainer to engage with the audience. Bring energy to your presentation! This group of people typically do not want to come to the program anyway. That is why incentives are needed to get them there. Trainers need to engage through their body language, tone of voice, hand gestures, etc. to NOT be BORING!

1. **Stand tall** and do not cross your legs, arms, or hands. (Have an open posture.)
2. **Talk clearly** and loud enough for everyone to hear you.
3. **Ask questions**. You want to hear from them.
4. **Do NOT use a monotone voice.**

Money & ME: Train the Trainer
2017© Money & ME, LLC All Rights Reserved

Dealing with Difficulties

There is no right or wrong answer to the following questions. However, you need to think through what you would do if these situations happen to you. Talk to your sponsoring organization about its policies, so you have an awareness of how to handle situations. Work individually and then as a group to answer the following questions.

1. What would you do if a person arrives intoxicated?

   _____

   _____

   _____

2. What difficult situations or personalities have you dealt with that may help you handle future situations?

   _____

   _____

   _____

3. What if more children show up and you don't have adequate childcare?

   _____

   _____

   _____

4. What if technology fails?

   _____

   _____

   _____

5. What if no one shows up?

   _____

   _____

6. What other problems should you anticipate?

   _____

   _____

NOTES:

6

Equipping the Coach / Mentor

- Coach's Mentor's Role
- Meeting Places and Times
- Who Should You Coach?
- What Does a Coach Do?
- Resources for Unusual Situations

What Is the Coach's Role?

- The Coach's role is to encourage and instruct. It is important to make sure there is not a conflict of interest.
- The *Money & ME Program* is not a forum to give financial advice.
- Coaches should find additional resources in the community to help with other needs.

Meeting Places and Times

- <u>Selecting the Follow-up Place</u>: The BEST place to meet is where you had the *Money & ME Program*. It is important to meet in a public setting and **not in a person's home**. Meeting at the host site will encourage people to return to the organization if they need more assistance because they have become familiar with the location.
- <u>Time</u>: Choose a time to meet with participants, preferably on a regular basis.

Faithful, Available, Teachable - "FAT" People

Your time is valuable! You have a limited number of hours in a day, and how you invest those hours is crucial. As you ponder who to give your time to, look for the following three qualities.

F - Faithful: Work with people who have already kept commitments they made. These are individuals who attended the orientation, workshop, and follow-up. They demonstrated that they are eager to learn.

A – Available: Coach people who have the time or will make the time to learn. If they are not available to meet with you, talk with them about it. Let them know you recognize they are very busy. When they can make adjustments in their schedules to meet with you, you would be happy to coach them. However, a Coach cannot make a person be available. A Coach should understand that not every person will be available, even though, as a Coach, you recognize this would be very valuable for him / her.

T – Teachable: Make sure the person is willing to learn and apply his / her knowledge.

Information from Chris Adsit, Associate National Director of Discipleship, Military Ministry

Credit Scores and Bankruptcy

Participants may want information on credit scores, bankruptcy, or consolidating their debt. This information is not included in the *Money & ME Program*. However, as a Trainer you should have information for these unusual situations. The following resources are included to assist you when helping the participant.

Credit Scores

Annual Credit Report is a free credit report every 12 months
Contact: www.annualcreditreport.com or call 1.800.322.8228

Bankruptcy

Do not advise a person on bankruptcy issues. Bankruptcy does not work for student loans, child or alimony support, or taxes within the past 3 years. If someone wants information, you can refer the person to call the State Bar Foundation in your state to see what is available. Some states have a free workshop.

Consolidating Debt

Credibility.org also known as ClearPoint
Has counselors who are available 24/7 by telephone and online to listen and answer your questions, in both English and Spanish. To speak with a counselor and schedule an in-person appointment, call 800.251.2227.

Trinity Debt Management
A non-profit agency, Trinity provides counseling and debt management services for individuals and families who are experiencing debt problems. Call 800.758.3844 or visit www.trinitycredit.org.

1. What is the purpose of a Coach?

_____

_____

_____

2. What does a Coach do?

_____

_____

_____

3. What are things a Coach should not do?

_____

_____

_____

4. What type of relationship should a Coach and participant have?

_____

_____

_____

5. What do you do if a participant needs more help than you can offer?

_____

_____

_____

6. What type of person should you work with?

_____

_____

_____

7

Forms

All forms available at with subscription to Money & ME University.

These forms are to assist you in planning and successful implementation of a *Money & ME Program*.

- Flyers: The flyers are in a fill-in format. You can add the location, date, time, notes, participation gifts / incentives, etc.
- Program Request: This is used for a trainer to request to have a program at a specific organization.
- Planning Checklist: To make sure everything is in place for a successful program.
- Volunteer Application: Anyone that will be helping with the Money & ME Program should complete this so the coordinator has everyone' s contact information.
- Trainer Registration: This is for everyone who will be a certified trainer.
- Trainer Evaluation: This is for people assisting with the program to give feedback to the lead trainer.
- Program Evaluation: This is for everyone who helped with the program to feedback (childcare workers, trainers, coaches, etc.)
- Sign In Sheets for participants and childcare.

Money & ME: Train the Trainer
2017© Money & ME, LLC All Rights Reserved

Planning Checklist

Timeline	Task	Name/Notes including contact information
Two months +	Identify Lead Trainer	
Two months +	Identify Assistant Trainer	
Two months+	Confirm approval for funding, dates at facility, and Trainer's availability	
6 weeks+	Make promotional flyers	
4 weeks+	Inform staff and / or congregation of program	
4 weeks+	Trainer to pick up PowerPoint to practice	
2 weeks +	Identify Childcare Worker #1 orientation	
2 weeks +	Identify Childcare Worker #2 orientation	
2 weeks +	Identify Childcare Worker #3 workshop	
2 weeks +	Identify Childcare Worker #4 workshop	
2 weeks +	Identify Facility person (person to open building and deal with facility issues)	
1-2 weeks	Distribute flyers in neighborhood	
1 week +	Confirm with clean-up crew: orientation	
1 week +	Confirm with clean-up crew: workshop	
1 week +	Obtain screen	
1 week +	Obtain projector, connection cord, power cord	
1 week +	Obtain extension cord	
1 week +	Obtain laptop computer and cord	
1 week +	Obtain clicker and extra batteries	
1 week +	Practice PowerPoint Presentation	
1 week +	Obtain camera (optional)	
1-2 days +	Identify who will provide snacks at orientation (i.e. granola bars, fruit, cheese/crackers, etc.)	
1-2 days +	Identify who will provide meal at workshop (i.e. sandwiches, Frito pie, casserole, etc.)	
1-2 days	Call participants	
1-2 days	Pick up workbooks, money kits & incentives	

56

# Volunteer Application

Date _____ Hosting Organization _____

Name _____ Birthday _____

Address _____

City _____ State _____ Zip Code_____

Home # _____ Cell # _____ Work # _____

Preferred E-mail *(home or work)* _____

Preferred Role(s): *check all that apply*

_____ Lead Trainer *(teacher presenting PowerPoint information)*
_____ Assistant Trainer *(administrative person)*
_____ Childcare Worker
_____ Coach
_____ Coordinator
_____ Promoter

How did you hear about the *Money & ME Program*? _____

Why would you like to be involved with the *Money & ME Program*? _____

_____

_____

Reference Name and Phone Number _____

Photographic Release: I grant the right to take photos and / or videos of my volunteer activities for promotional purposes. Initials _____

Background Check (if needed): I hereby authorize _____ and its designated agents and representatives to conduct a comprehensive review of my background causing a consumer report and / or an investigative consumer report for volunteer purposes. I understand that the scope of the consumer report may include, but is not limited to, the following areas: verification of Social Security number, current residence, employment history, education, character references, drug testing, civil and criminal history records from any criminal justice agency in any or all federal, state, and county jurisdictions, driving records, birth records, and any other public records. Initials _____

The information in this application is correct to the best of my knowledge.

Signature _____

Money & ME: Train the Trainer
2017© Money & ME, LLC All Rights Reserved

Trainer Evaluation

(This is for a Money & ME Helper to fill out to give feedback for the Lead Trainer. Not for participants to fill out.)

Location _____ Program Dates _____

Trainer _____ Evaluation completed by _____

It is important to give constructive feedback to the Trainer. *Money & ME* encourages that this be done after the orientation and before the workshop. That way if something needs to be corrected, there is an opportunity to do so.

Trainer	Great	Adequate	Needs Attention
Comfortable with technology			
Knowledge of program			
Engaged with audience			
Professional			
Able to control class			
Encouraged participants			

List three things that the Trainer *did REALLY well during this program*.

_____

_____

_____

Needs Attention: *If you felt something needed attention, please write down what happened and ideas for improvement.*

_____

_____

_____

_____

_____

Other thoughts / comments:

_____

_____

Program Evaluation

(This is for people who helped with the Money & ME program to complete to improve program. Not for participants to fill out.)

Location _____ Program Dates _____

It is important to schedule a debriefing time for the Trainers and Coordinators. Feedback from everyone is a critical part of this process. Make sure everyone has a copy of this program evaluation and completes it prior to the debriefing. Note: Not everyone needs to attend the debriefing, but everyone needs to complete this evaluation.

Name _____ Program Role _____

	Great	Adequate	Needs Attention
Facility			
Promotion / Attendance			
Food			
Childcare			
Lead Trainer			
Assistant Trainer			
Program Coordinator			
Coach(es)			
Program Dates & Times			

Positive outcomes of program: *Please describe from your perspective 1-3 things that the team did REALLY well during this program.*

_____

_____

Needs Attention: *If you felt something needed more attention, please write down what happened and ideas for improvement.*

_____

_____

Areas to improve: *Please describe from your perspective 1-3 things that the organization's leadership could do to improve future programs.*

_____

_____

Program Content: *Money & ME welcomes your feedback. Keep us informed about your program and tell us your suggestions. E-mail contactus@MoneyandME.cash.*

_____

8

Bibliography

Bibles Used
- New International Version – NIV
- New American Standard Bible – NASB
- Holman Christian Standard Bible – HCSB
- English Standard Version – ESV

Difficult Personalities
DiResta, Diane. *"How to Handle Difficult Audiences."*
http://www.diresta.com/resources/articles/how-to-handle-difficult-audiences/

Engaging the Audience
Freifeld, Lorri. *"7 Secrets to Engaging an Audience."* January 22, 2013.
www.trainingmag.com/content/7-secrets-engaging-audience.

Gambling
Quinn, James. American's Gambling $100 Billion in Casino's Like Rats in a Cage. October 11, 2009. www.marketoracle.co.uk/Article14128.html.

Mentoring
Adsit, Chris. *"Discipling FAT People."*
http://www.disciplemakersinternational.org/free/articles/article016.htm

Other Ways to be Wealthy
Mahon, Rob. Navigators, Faith at Work Luncheons, 2014-2015, Albuquerque, New Mexico

Payment Plan
Debt-snowball method, https://en.wikipedia.org/wiki/Debt-snowball_method

Public Speaking Tips
Toastmasters.org

Recipes for cleaning products
www.pinterest.com

Understanding Poverty
Payne, Ruby. *A Framework for Understanding Poverty: A Cognitive Approach (5th Revised Edition) Highlands, TX: aha! Process, Inc., 2013.*

Made in the USA
San Bernardino, CA
26 May 2017